Date: 3/19/19

J 745.5 YAT
Yates, Jane,
Sensational bird crafts /

Sensational

BIRD Crafts

Jane Yates

Gareth Stevens
PUBLISHING

Published in 2019 by Gareth Stevens,
an Imprint of Rosen Publishing
29 East 21st Street, New York, NY 10010

Developed and produced for Rosen by BlueAppleWorks Inc.

Creative Director: Melissa McClellan
Managing Editor for BlueAppleWorks: Melissa McClellan
Designer: T.J. Choleva
Photo Research: Jane Reid
Editor: Marcia Abramson

Craft Artisans: Jane Yates (p. 8, 10, 12, 14, 16, 18, 20, 22, 24, 26, 28)

Photo Credits: © cover center Nakorn Vipattanaporn/Dreamstime ; cover top left Austen Photography; cover top right Austen Photography; cover middle rightAusten Photography; cover bottom right Austen Photography; Paw print Dreamzdesigners/Shutterstock.com; p. 4 left David Ryo/Shutterstock.com; p 4 top right BestPhotoStudio/Shutterstock.com; p. 4 top right middle Zurijeta/Shutterstock.com; p. 4 bottom right middle Zurijeta/Shutterstock.com; p. 4 bottom right Kalinina Alisa/Shutterstock.com; p. 5 top left kurhan/Shutterstock.com; p. 5 middle left Vyaseleva Elena/Shutterstock.com; p. 5 bottom left Nick Beer/Shutterstock.com; p. 5 top right Kharkhan Oleg /Shutterstock.com; p. 5 bottom right Thomas Skjaeveland/Shutterstock.com; p. 6, 17 MongPro/Shutterstock.com; p. 7 Butterfly Hunter/Shutterstock.com; p. 9, 29 cynoclub/Shutterstock.com; p. 11 prapass/Shutterstock.com; p. 21, 25 Africa Studio/Shutterstock.com; p. 24 photomaster/Shutterstock.com; p. 27 vitals/Shutterstock.com; p. 32 left BESTWEB/Shutterstock.com; p. 32 right razorbeam/Shutterstock.com; back cover left to right: Africa Studio/Shutterstock.com; Drozhzhina Elena/Shutterstock.com; apichon_tee/Shutterstock.com; Tracy Starr/Shutterstock.com; All craft photography Austen Photography

Cataloging-in-Publication-Data
Names: Yates, Jane.
Title: Sensational bird crafts / Jane Yates.
Description: New York : Gareth Stevens Publishing, 2019. | Series: Get crafty with pets! | Includes glossary and index.
Identifiers: LCCN ISBN 9781538226278 (pbk.) | ISBN 9781538226261 (library bound) | ISBN 9781538226285 (6 pack)
Subjects: LCSH: Handicraft--Juvenile literature. | Cage birds as pets--Juvenile literature. | Pets--Juvenile literature. | Pet supplies--Juvenile literature.
Classification: LCC TT160.Y38 2019 | DDC 745.59--dc23

Manufactured in the United States of America

CPSIA Compliance Information: Batch #CS18GS For Further Information contact: Rosen Publishing, New York, New York at 1-800-237-9932

Contents

Birds as Pets

Birds are the third most popular pet after dogs and cats. Most pet birds are members of the parrot species. The most common pet birds are budgerigars, also known as parakeets or budgies, lovebirds, and cockatiels. Large parrots such as cockatoos, African greys, and Amazons are also kept as pets but are less common. Non-parrot pet birds are finches and canaries. They are less social and often don't like to interact with people.

Birds can make great pets. If you handle and get them used to people when they are very young, they can be quite friendly and enjoy interacting with you. With patience and treats you can even train them.

Birds are adorable and very fun to watch. They do need toys and ways of exercising, such as getting time out of their cage to fly. They like to sing and chirp, and some can even talk!

Birds make good pets. They can be very shy at first. You have to earn their trust and love by treating them with kindness and taking good care of them.

BIRDS MAKE US HAPPY

BIRDS LOVE ATTENTION

BIRDS ARE FASCINATING TO WATCH

BIRD PHOTOGRAPHY

You might want to take pictures of your pet bird and use them for some craft projects. Read the tips below and try taking pictures of your bird.

Make sure your bird feels comfortable. Take photos on the animal's level—don't take all the photos from above. It's best to take the photos near a window. Use treats and a squeaky toy to make your bird look at you. Take lots of pictures from different angles. If you take your bird out of the cage for photos, make sure it is a safe area and you have a helper to watch the bird while you take photos.

EYE LEVEL

CLOSE-UP

HIGH ANGLE

ACTION

LOW ANGLE

PHOTO TIP
Take photos when your bird is out of its cage for playtime.

Techniques

These projects are great for bird lovers, whether you have a bird now or hope to have a bird in the future (make and save the toys in a bird **hope chest**). When making toys, adjust the size to fit your bird. Larger birds require larger toys. Most of the materials in this book can be easily found. You may have some already. Others can be purchased at craft or dollar stores. Use the following techniques to create your crafts.

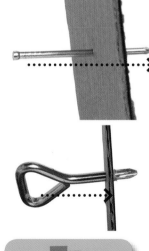

PAPER-MACHE GLUE

> Add 1 cup (250 ml) of white glue and ⅓ cup (80 ml) of water in a bowl. Mix the glue and water together with a spoon. If you have leftover glue, put it in a container with a lid and use it later. (An empty yogurt container works well.)

MAKING HOLES IN CARDBOARD

Some projects require holes to be made in cardboard.

> Small holes — push a nail through the cardboard. Always point the nail away from yourself!

> Big holes — start with the nail to make a small hole, then push a Phillips screwdriver through the small hole to make it larger. Then insert your scissors and cut the hole to the size you want.

TIP

Use only nontoxic glue and food coloring on any toy you make for a bird.

A NOTE ABOUT MEASUREMENTS

Measurements are given in U.S. form with metric in parentheses. The metric conversion is rounded to the nearest whole number to make it easier to measure.

TIP

Introduce toys carefully to your bird. Birds can be shy with a new toy and may need a day or two to accept it. After that, keep a close eye on how your bird plays with it. Never leave a bird alone with a toy unless you are certain it is safe.

Larks Head Knot

> Use a larks head knot to attach one string to a dowel, rope, or another piece of string.

> Fold the string in half. Place the loop just below the other string.

> Bring the two ends of the string down and through the loop.

> Pull the two ends tight to make the knot.

Bowline Knot

> A bowline knot is a good knot for attaching string or rope to another object such as a **carabiner.**

> Make a loop.

> Bring the **working end** of the string through the underside of the loop.

> Wrap the end of the string around the standing piece of string and back through the loop.

> Hold the standing piece of the string and tighten the knot by pulling on the free end of the string.

Overhand Knot

> The overhand knot is a simple knot often used to secure beads in crafts.

> Make a loop with the string.

> Bring the working end of the string through the loop by going under the loop and then over the loop.

> Pull the working end to tighten.

BE PREPARED

> Read through the instructions and make sure you have all the materials you need.

> Clean up when you are finished making your crafts. Put away your supplies for next time.

BE SAFE

> Ask for help when you need it.

> Ask for permission to borrow tools.

> Be careful when using scissors and nails.

Treat Ball

Your bird will have fun with this cardboard treat ball.

Tools & Materials:

✔ Cardboard tube
✔ Ruler and scissors
✔ Bird treats
✔ Crinkled paper
✔ Twine

1. Cut a cardboard tube into five ¾-inch-wide (2 cm) loops. Flatten the tube slightly to make it easier to cut. Unflatten the loops after they are cut.

2. Place one loop inside the center of another loop.

3. Place a third loop over the other two.

4. Put some treats inside. Put some crinkled paper inside.

5. Place the fourth loop over the others. Spread them out so the treats don't fall out.

6. Tie a piece of twine to one of the loops. Tie the other end to your bird's cage.

Insert

Cut five loops

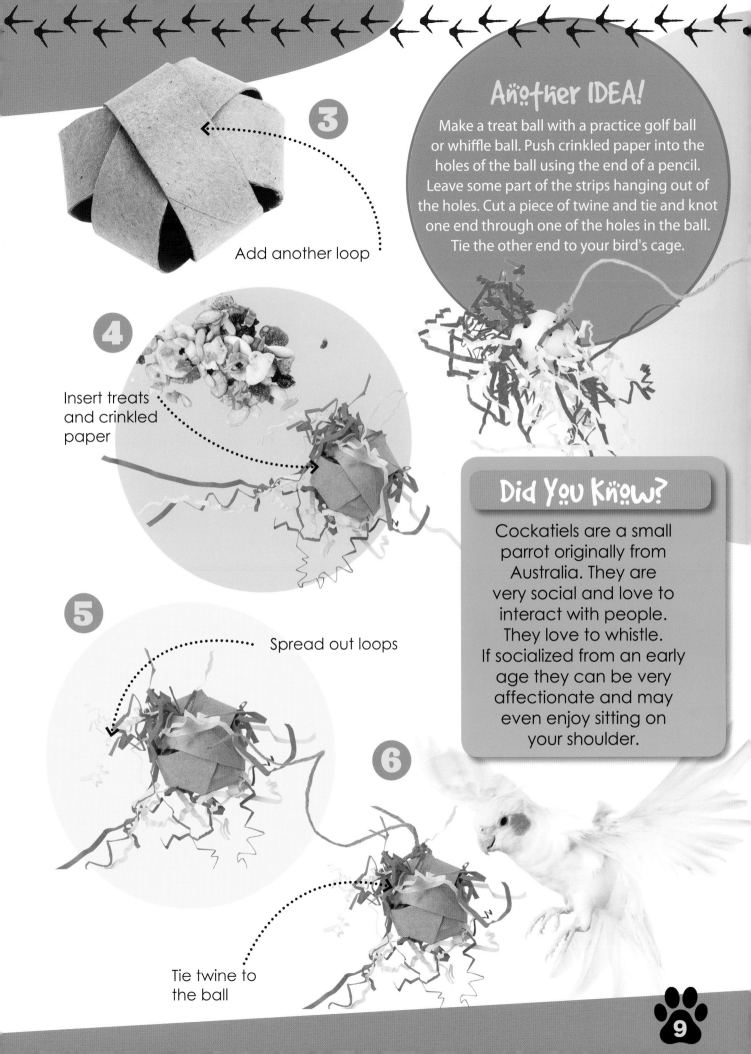

3

Add another loop

Another IDEA!

Make a treat ball with a practice golf ball or whiffle ball. Push crinkled paper into the holes of the ball using the end of a pencil. Leave some part of the strips hanging out of the holes. Cut a piece of twine and tie and knot one end through one of the holes in the ball. Tie the other end to your bird's cage.

4

Insert treats and crinkled paper

Did You Know?

Cockatiels are a small parrot originally from Australia. They are very social and love to interact with people. They love to whistle. If socialized from an early age they can be very affectionate and may even enjoy sitting on your shoulder.

5

Spread out loops

6

Tie twine to the ball

Felt Bird

Make a cute felt bird.

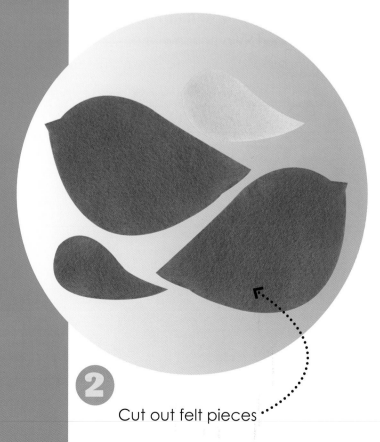

Tools & Materials:

- ✔ Paper and pencil
- ✔ Scissors
- ✔ Felt
- ✔ Tape and glue
- ✔ Black marker
- ✔ Small googly eye
- ✔ Sequins
- ✔ Ribbon
- ✔ Feathers

1. Trace the bird pattern pieces on page 31 onto a piece of paper. Cut out the pattern.

2. Tape the pieces to felt. Cut out all the pieces.

3. Use a black marker to color the beak on one of the bird shapes. Glue a small googly eye. Glue a heart sequin, or a small heart could be cut from felt and glued.

4. Glue sequins to the smaller wing. Glue the smaller wing to the larger wing.

5. Cut a small piece of ribbon. Glue the two ends together. Glue to the back of the bird. Glue a few feathers to the back of the bird.

6. Glue the other bird shape to the back.

7. Glue the wing to the front.

2

Cut out felt pieces

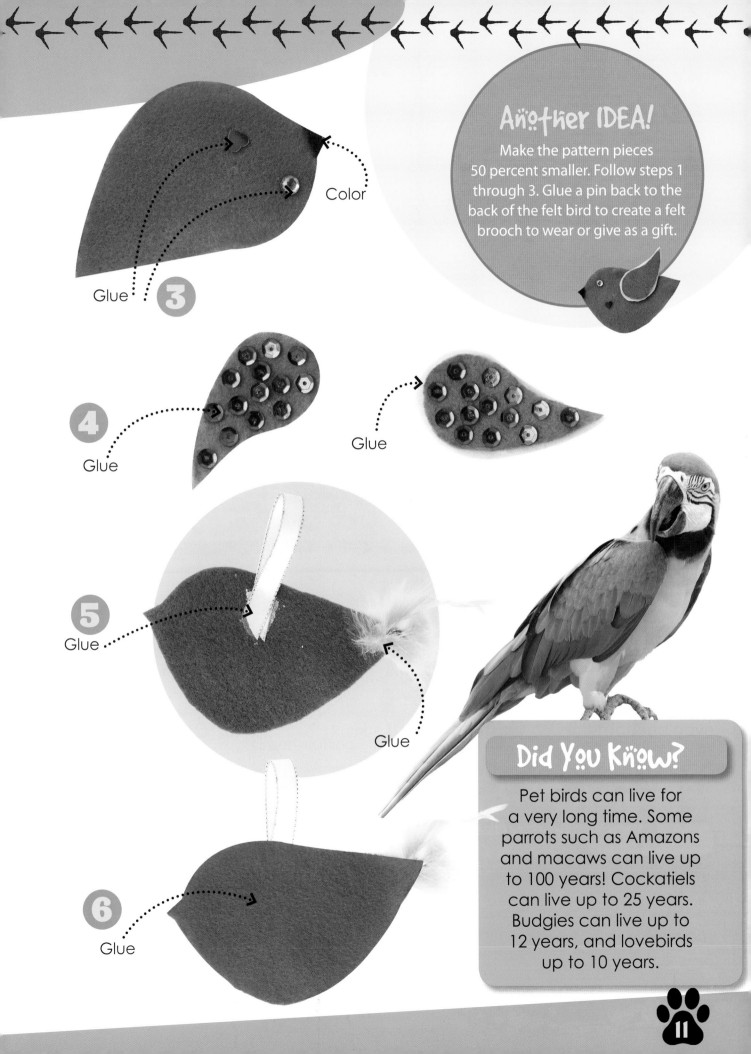

Color

Glue **3**

Another IDEA!

Make the pattern pieces 50 percent smaller. Follow steps 1 through 3. Glue a pin back to the back of the felt bird to create a felt brooch to wear or give as a gift.

4

Glue

Glue

5

Glue

Glue

6

Glue

Did You Know?

Pet birds can live for a very long time. Some parrots such as Amazons and macaws can live up to 100 years! Cockatiels can live up to 25 years. Budgies can live up to 12 years, and lovebirds up to 10 years.

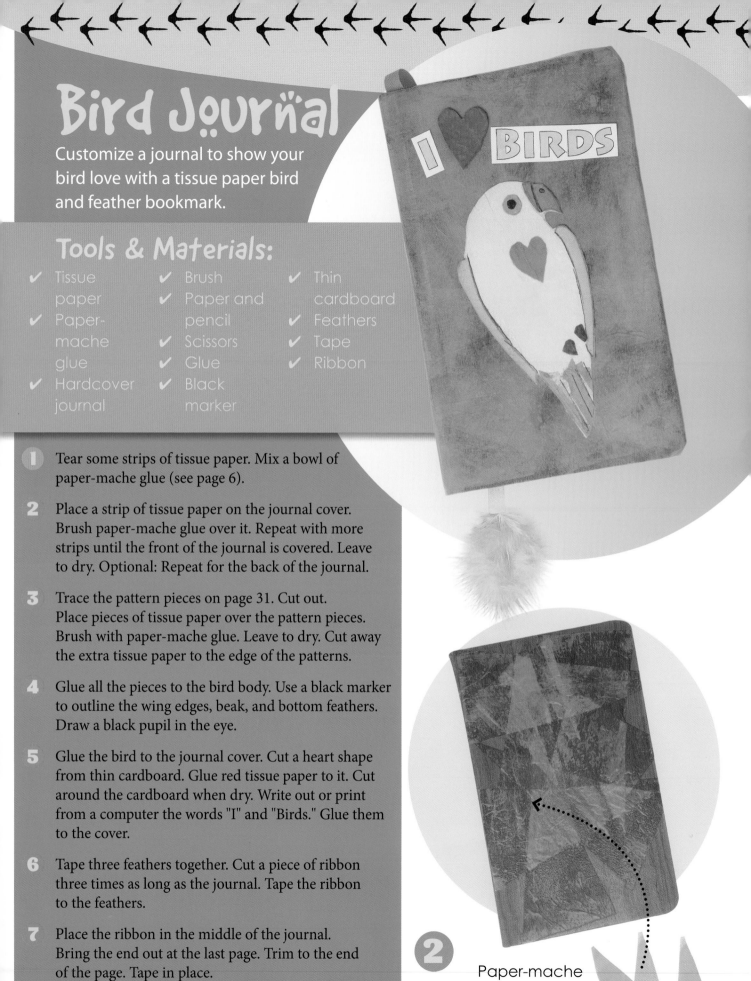

Bird Journal

Customize a journal to show your bird love with a tissue paper bird and feather bookmark.

Tools & Materials:

- ✔ Tissue paper
- ✔ Paper-mache glue
- ✔ Hardcover journal
- ✔ Brush
- ✔ Paper and pencil
- ✔ Scissors
- ✔ Glue
- ✔ Black marker
- ✔ Thin cardboard
- ✔ Feathers
- ✔ Tape
- ✔ Ribbon

1. Tear some strips of tissue paper. Mix a bowl of paper-mache glue (see page 6).

2. Place a strip of tissue paper on the journal cover. Brush paper-mache glue over it. Repeat with more strips until the front of the journal is covered. Leave to dry. Optional: Repeat for the back of the journal.

3. Trace the pattern pieces on page 31. Cut out. Place pieces of tissue paper over the pattern pieces. Brush with paper-mache glue. Leave to dry. Cut away the extra tissue paper to the edge of the patterns.

4. Glue all the pieces to the bird body. Use a black marker to outline the wing edges, beak, and bottom feathers. Draw a black pupil in the eye.

5. Glue the bird to the journal cover. Cut a heart shape from thin cardboard. Glue red tissue paper to it. Cut around the cardboard when dry. Write out or print from a computer the words "I" and "Birds." Glue them to the cover.

6. Tape three feathers together. Cut a piece of ribbon three times as long as the journal. Tape the ribbon to the feathers.

7. Place the ribbon in the middle of the journal. Bring the end out at the last page. Trim to the end of the page. Tape in place.

2 Paper-mache the cover

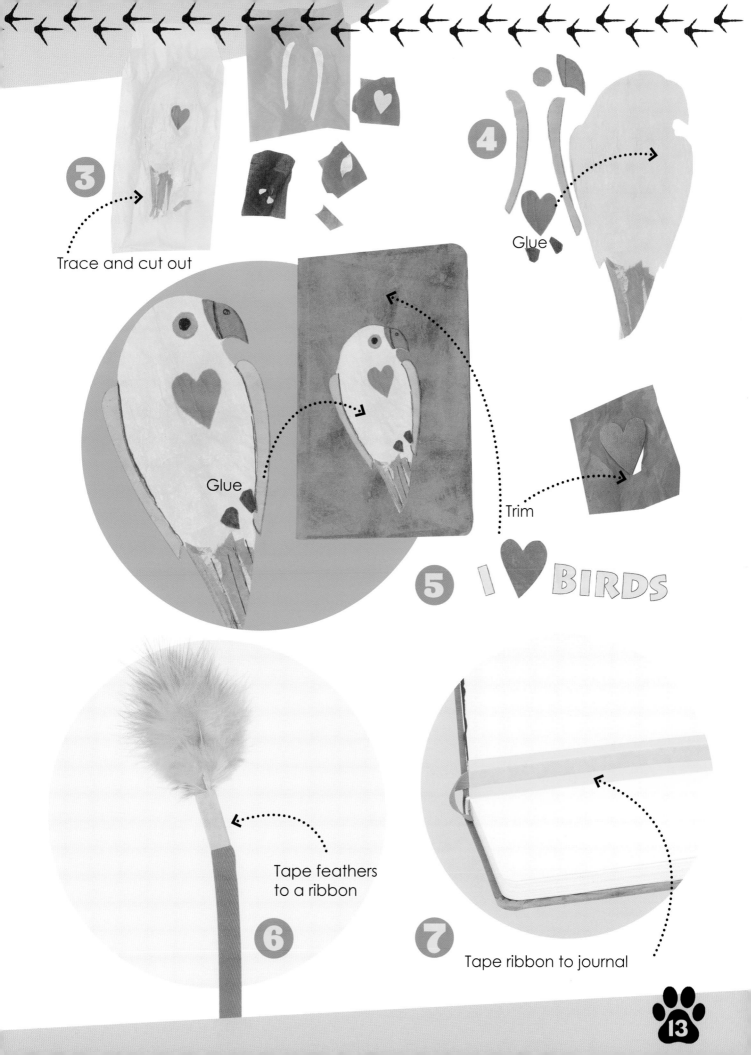

3 Trace and cut out

4 Glue

5 I ❤ BIRDS

Glue

Trim

6 Tape feathers to a ribbon

7 Tape ribbon to journal

13

Pom-Pom Bird

Make an adorable pom-pom bird. Or make two or three!

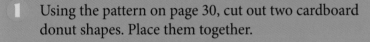

Tools & Materials:

✔ Corrugated cardboard
✔ Paper and pencil
✔ Bulky yarn (or use four strands at a time for thinner yarn)
✔ Scissors
✔ Felt
✔ Glue
✔ Googly eyes

1 Using the pattern on page 30, cut out two cardboard donut shapes. Place them together.

2 Start winding the yarn around the donut. Wind a thick layer. The more yarn, the thicker the pom-pom. If you run out of yarn, just start winding a new strand. You can add a new color if you want.

3 Place scissors between the two cardboard donuts and cut the yarn.

4 Cut a piece of yarn and wind it between the two cardboard donuts. Pull the yarn tight and make a double knot. Remove the cardboard. Trim the pom-pom so it is even.

5 Cut out the pattern pieces using the pattern on page 30. Cut the feet from cardboard. Cut the other pattern pieces from felt. Glue the cardboard feet to the pom-pom. Glue the wings and tail felt pieces to the pom-pom.

6 Fold the beak piece in half and glue below the eyes. Glue the googly eyes to the pom-pom.

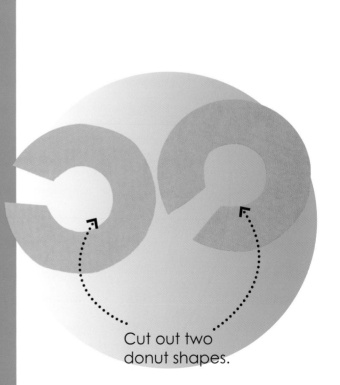

Cut out two donut shapes.

1

2

Wind around the cardboard.

3

Cut

Did You Know?

Birds like to hang out together. They are very social and live in groups called flocks. This is true for budgerigars and even the large parrots. A flock of parrots is sometimes called a pandemonium, which is probably what they sound like!

Trim

4

Tie

5

Glue

6

Fold and glue

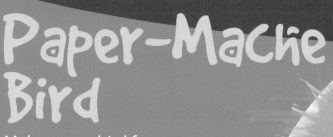

Paper-Mache Bird

Make a cute bird from paper-mache.

Tools & Materials:

✔ Styrofoam balls (1 small, 1 medium)
✔ Toothpicks
✔ Scissors
✔ Paper
✔ Masking tape
✔ Paper-mache glue
✔ Paper towel
✔ Acrylic or poster paint
✔ Paintbrush
✔ Feathers
✔ Glue
✔ Googly eyes

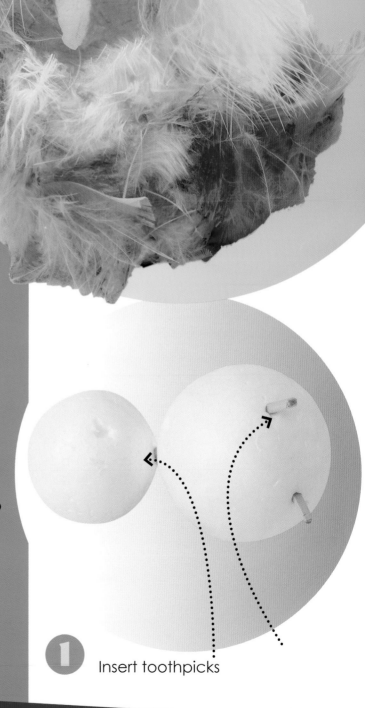

1. Stick a toothpick into the smaller Styrofoam ball. Push the other end into the larger ball. Break a toothpick in half and stick each of the broken ends into the bottom of the larger ball.

2. Cut wings and a tail shape from paper. Cover with masking tape.

3. Tape to the body.

4. Mix the paper-mache glue (see page 6) and begin to cover the bird with strips of paper towel dipped in the glue. Make a beak shape by rolling one strip into a ball. Press it into the head and shape it to look like a beak. Let dry overnight.

5. When the bird is dry, cover the whole bird with acrylic or poster paint. Let the bird dry.

6. Decorate your bird by gluing feathers to it. Glue googly eyes above the beak.

1 Insert toothpicks

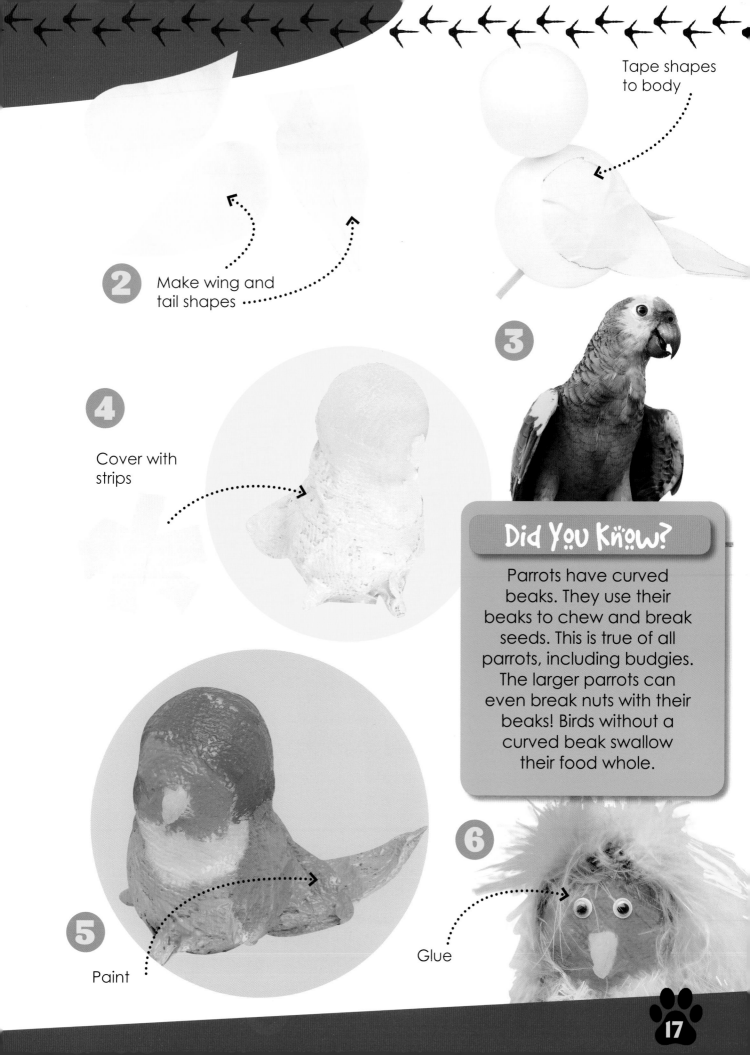

Tape shapes to body

2 Make wing and tail shapes

3

4 Cover with strips

Did You Know?

Parrots have curved beaks. They use their beaks to chew and break seeds. This is true of all parrots, including budgies. The larger parrots can even break nuts with their beaks! Birds without a curved beak swallow their food whole.

5 Paint

6 Glue

Spinning and Stacking Toy

Make a colorful spinning and stacking toy for your bird.

Tools & Materials:

- ✔ Nail
- ✔ Craft sticks
- ✔ Corrugated cardboard
- ✔ Glue
- ✔ Straws
- ✔ Scissors
- ✔ Beads
- ✔ Cotton rope or twine
- ✔ Bell
- ✔ Branch or dowel
- ✔ Carabiner

1. Use a nail to poke a hole in the center of 9 craft sticks.

2. Cut some rectangle shapes from corrugated cardboard. Fold them into thirds. Poke a hole through the center. Use a small amount of glue to glue them together.

3. Cut three straws in half. Use a nail to poke a hole in the center of each of the half straws

4. Select some beads to add to the toy.

5. Cut a piece of rope or twine. It should be double the size you want the finished size to be. Tie the rope to the bell and make a knot. Attach the bell to the branch or dowel using the larks head knot (see page 7).

6. Start threading the beads, craft sticks, straws, and cardboard pieces onto the rope.

7. When you have all the pieces on the rope, loop the rope through a carabiner and tie using a bowline knot (see page 7).

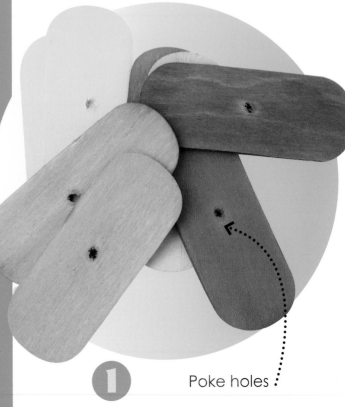

1

Poke holes

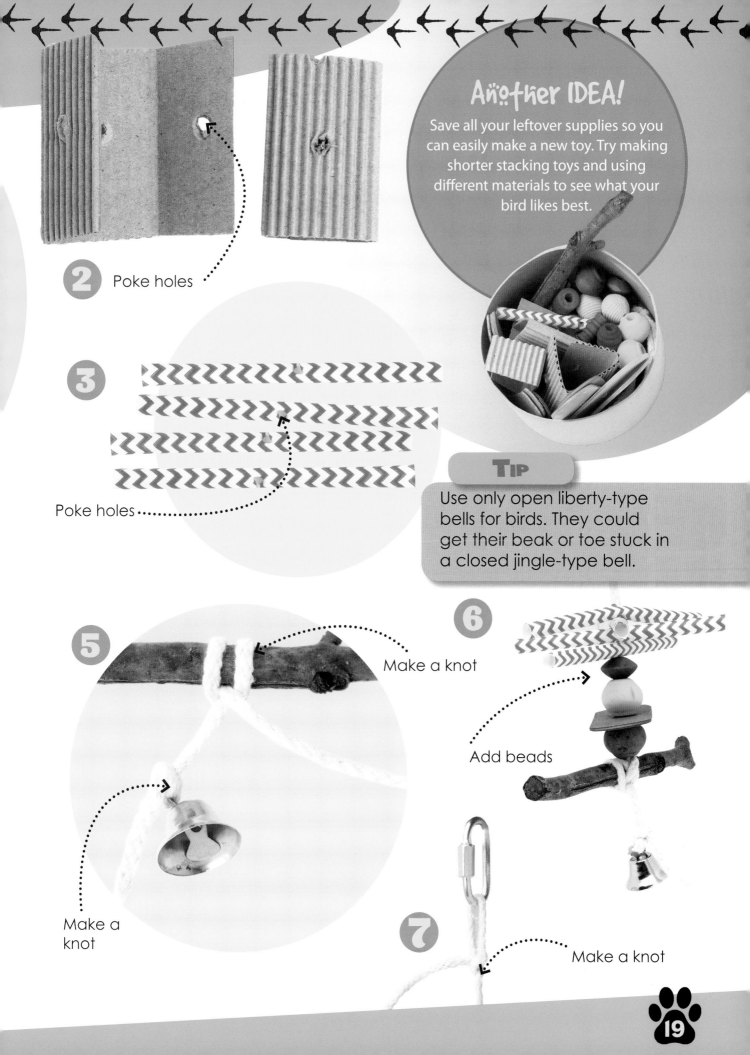

2 Poke holes

3 Poke holes

Another IDEA!

Save all your leftover supplies so you can easily make a new toy. Try making shorter stacking toys and using different materials to see what your bird likes best.

TIP

Use only open liberty-type bells for birds. They could get their beak or toe stuck in a closed jingle-type bell.

5 Make a knot

Make a knot

6 Add beads

Make a knot

7 Make a knot

Treat Jar

Make jars to store bird treats or give as a gift—or even to store your own treats or treasures!

Tools & Materials:

- ✔ Jar
- ✔ Glue
- ✔ Plastic or paper cup
- ✔ Acrylic paint
- ✔ Paintbrush
- ✔ Paper and pencil
- ✔ Markers or colored pencils
- ✔ Scissors
- ✔ Paper-mache glue
- ✔ Permanent markers
- ✔ Tissue paper

1. Pour a small amount of glue into a plastic or paper cup. Add some paint. Stir. Add more paint until you are happy with the color. (The glue helps the paint stick to the jar.)

2. Paint the jar and leave to dry.

3. Use the pattern on page 31 to draw and color paper birds with markers or colored pencils. Cut the birds out. (Don't cut the legs.) Print the word "treats." Cut out.

4. Prepare a small bowl of paper-mache glue. (See page 6.) Apply some glue to the jar. Press an image into the glue. Smooth out. Repeat with each image you want to put on the jar. Draw the legs and feet with a **permanent marker.**

5. Brush glue around the top and side of the lid. Wrap tissue paper around the lid. Leave to dry. When it's dry, trim the extra tissue paper away. Glue a paper bird to the top of the lid. Glue a treats label.

2 Paint the jar

3

treats

Color

Cut out

treats

Another IDEA!

Trace the bird patterns on page 31. Cut the paper out roughly following the shape of the bird. Tape each bird to the inside of a jar. Using a permanent marker, trace around the bird on the outside of the jar. Use color markers to color the birds. Remove the paper from inside the jar.

treats

4

Glue images

Draw legs and feet

treats

5

Trim

Glue images

treats

Did You Know?

Parrots will eat almost anything. They eat seeds, fruits, and vegetables. In the wild they will eat insects as well. Most birdseed mixes include safflower seeds, sunflower seeds, millet seeds, canary seeds, hemp seeds, thistle seeds, and more.

climbing Net

Make a climbing net. Hang it in the cage or on a wall if your bird has cage-free time.

Tools & Materials:

✔ Twine (shown in color to make it easier to follow)
✔ Scissors
✔ Pony beads

1. Cut two pieces of twine 12 inches (30 cm) long. Cut six pieces 48 inches (122 cm) long. Set one of the 12-inch (30 cm) pieces aside.

2. Tie the six pieces to one of the short pieces using larks head knots (see page 7). Space them out leaving extra twine on either side for tying the net to the cage.

3. Pull each outside string away from the others. Join the next two strings and make a knot about an inch (3 cm) from the top. Repeat with the rest of the strings.

4. On the next row, join the outside strings in when making knots. Alternate leaving the outside strings in and out when tying knots.

5. Add in **pony beads** by threading them onto the two strings before tying the knot.

6. To finish the net, tie each individual string to the other short string. Use the overhand knot (see page 7). Tie a few overhand knots, add a bead, and then a few more overhand knots. Trim the ends.

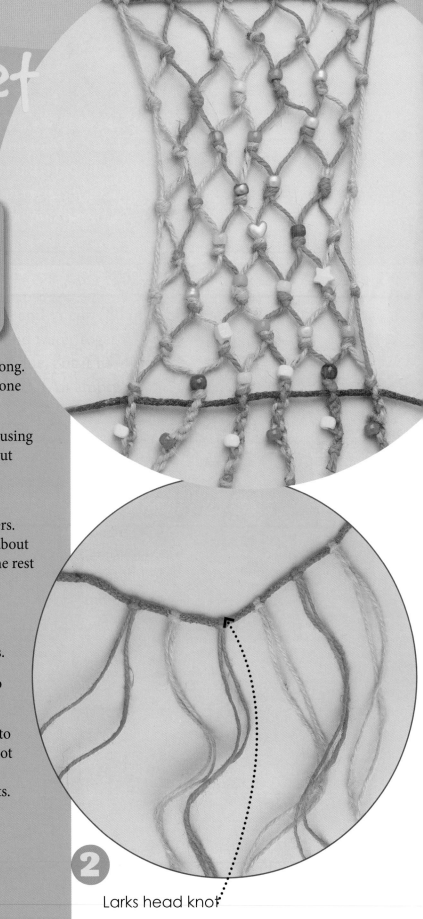

Larks head knot

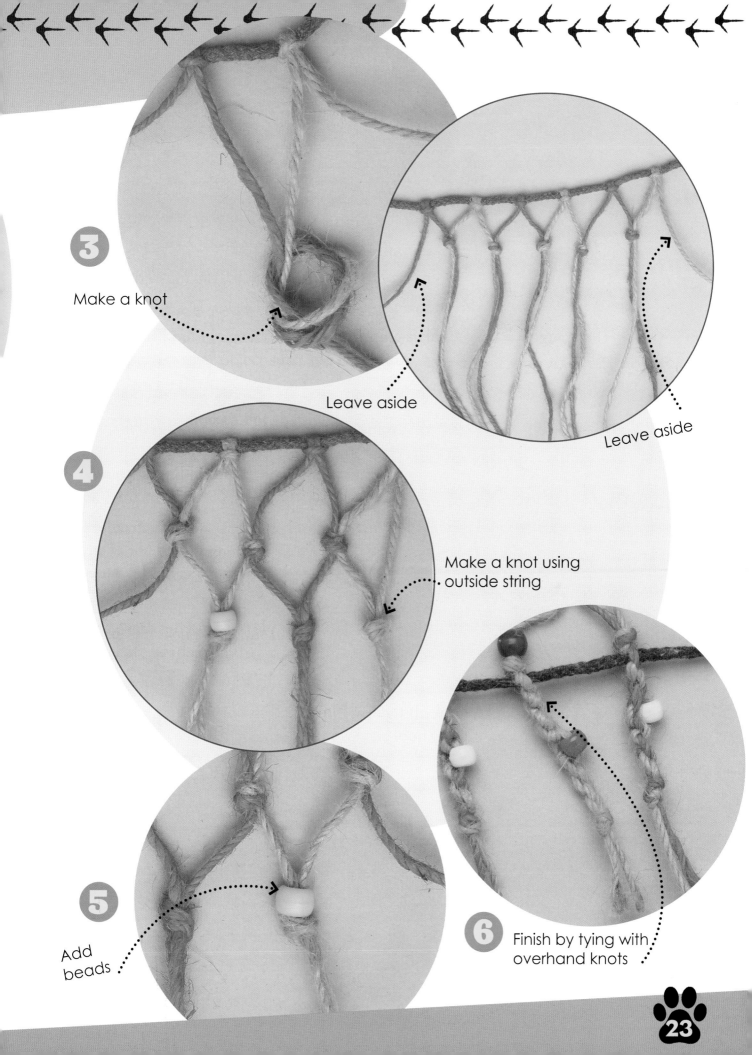

3 Make a knot

Leave aside

Leave aside

4 Make a knot using outside string

5 Add beads

6 Finish by tying with overhand knots

23

Swing Toy

Make a cute bird swing. Your bird can swing on it or use it as a perch to sit on.

Tools & Materials:

✔ Beads
✔ Craft wire (if using thin wire, use a double strand)
✔ Scissors and ruler
✔ Branch 6 inches (15 cm) long
✔ Carabiner

1. Select the beads you want to use. The beads can be wood beads or plastic pony beads.

2. Cut a piece of craft wire 18 inches (46 cm) long. Bend it in half. Bend the middle twice to make a loop.

3. Thread beads onto each side of the loop. (You may find it easier to do one side at a time.) Leave 3 inches (8 cm) clear on each side.

4. Wrap one end of the wire around the branch. (See page 31 for a list of bird-safe branches.) Wrap the other end around the opposite end of the branch.

5. Attach a carabiner through the loop. Attach the other end of the carabiner to the birdcage.

Select beads

24

2 Make a loop

Another IDEA!

Make the swing with a dowel. Bend a piece of craft wire in half. Make a loop in the middle. Thread pony beads onto each half of the wire. Wrap the ends around the dowel.

3 Add beads

Did You Know?

Birds can see a wide range of colors, even more than people can. Their vision is their most used sense. They hunt and forage for food using their keen eyesight. Some parrots even have preferences or dislikes for certain colors.

4 Wrap around

5 Attach carabiner

25

Mirror Toy

Make a mirror for your bird. Hold it so your pet can see its reflection.

Tools & Materials:

- ✔ Balsa wood or craft sticks 4 inches (10 cm) long
- ✔ Glue
- ✔ Jumbo craft sticks
- ✔ Straw
- ✔ Scissors and ruler
- ✔ Square mirror 3 inches (8 cm)
- ✔ Glue (nontoxic)
- ✔ Scissors

1. Make a base for the mirror. Glue four pieces of balsa wood and/or craft sticks together.

2. Glue six jumbo craft sticks to the frame.

3. Glue five jumbo craft sticks to the other craft sticks going in the opposite direction.

4. Cut a straw so that you have two 3-inch (8 cm) pieces and two 2¼-inch (6 cm) pieces. Cut each straw piece down the middle to make a slit.

5. Slip the longer straws over two edges of the mirror. Slip the shorter straws over the opposite side edges.

6. Put glue along the bottom of the straws and glue to the craft stick base.

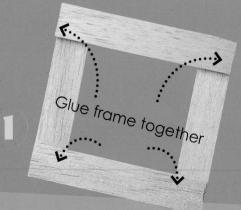

1 Glue frame together

2 Glue

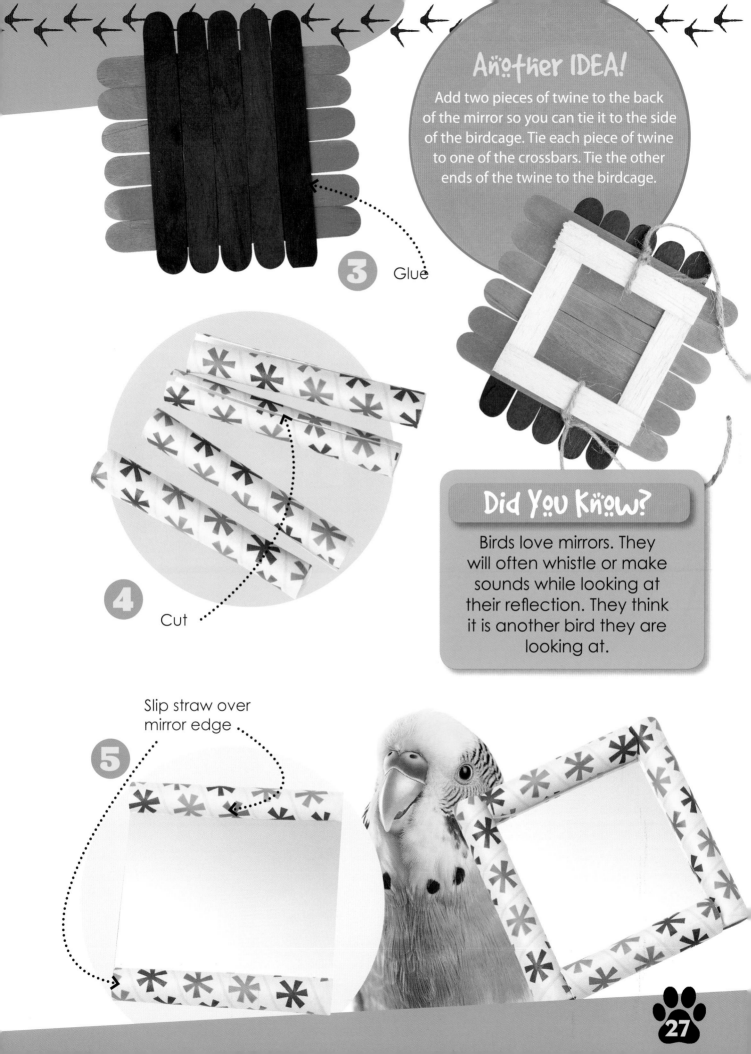

3 Glue

4 Cut

Slip straw over mirror edge

5

Foraging Toy

Make a pretty heart foraging toy for your bird.

Tools & Materials:

- ✔ Heart-shaped cardboard box (or square box)
- ✔ Nail
- ✔ Twine
- ✔ Food coloring
- ✔ Small paper cup
- ✔ Brush
- ✔ Beads
- ✔ Crinkled paper
- ✔ Glue

1 Use a nail to make holes along the side of the box. Make the holes below where the lid will sit. Make one hole at the top of the box.

2 Cut a piece of twine to hang the toy with. Make a double knot and thread the other end through the top hole.

3 Mix a few drops of food coloring with a tablespoon (15 ml) of water in a small paper cup. Brush the box lid with the food coloring.

4 Cut two short pieces of twine. Make a double knot at one end of each. Thread beads on the twine. Make another knot after the beads.

5 Thread the end of the twine through holes on the bottom of the box. Tie the two pieces of twine together and make a double knot.

6 Fill the box with crinkled paper. Push some through the holes.

7 Put some glue on the inside edge of the lid. Put the lid on the box. When the glue is dry, tie the toy to the birdcage.

1 Poke a hole

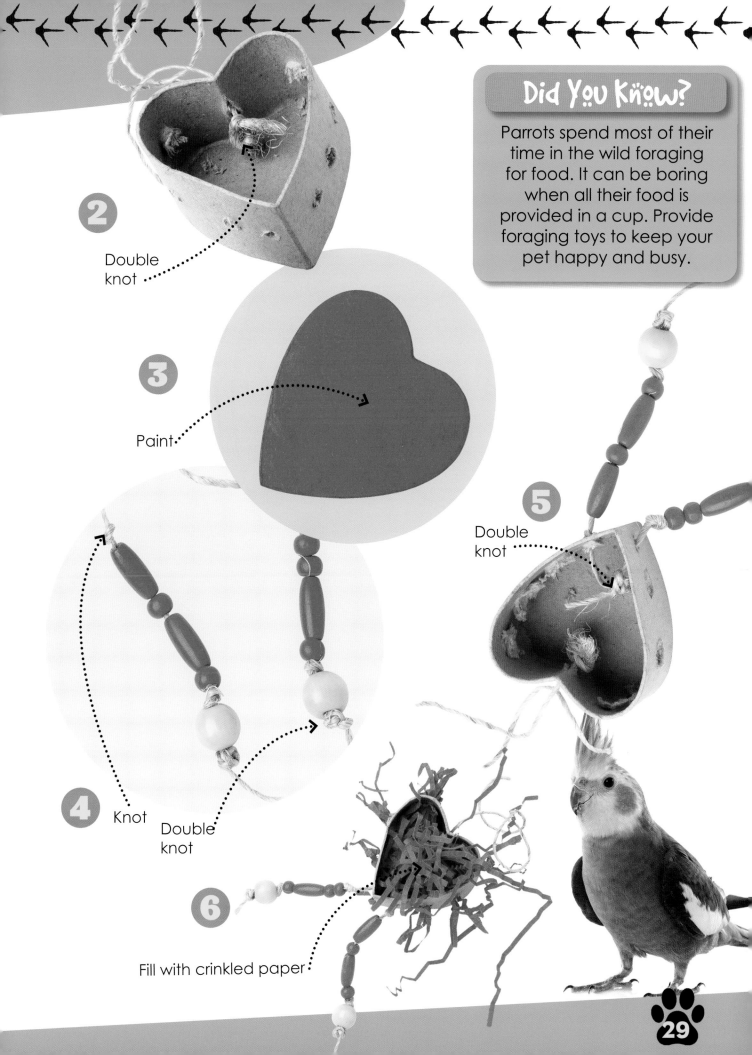

2 Double knot

Did You Know?

Parrots spend most of their time in the wild foraging for food. It can be boring when all their food is provided in a cup. Provide foraging toys to keep your pet happy and busy.

3 Paint

4 Knot

Double knot

5 Double knot

6 Fill with crinkled paper

Patterns

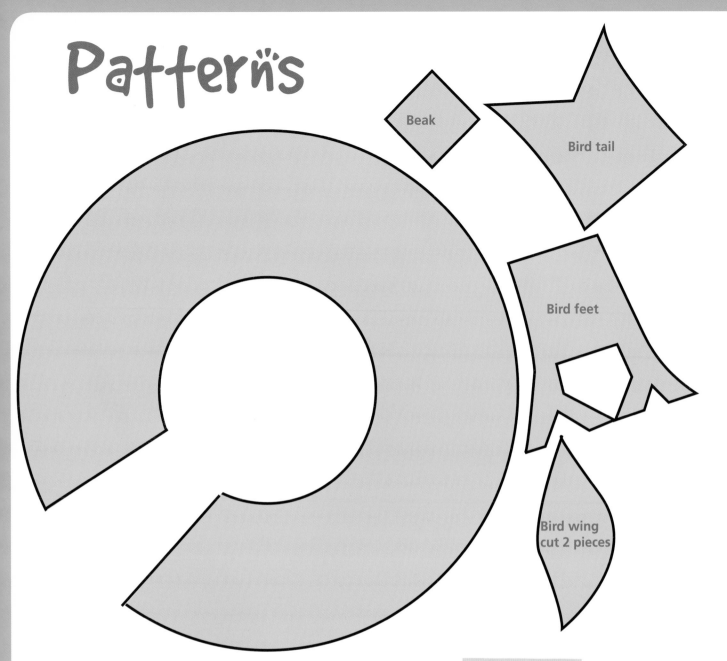

Beak

Bird tail

Bird feet

Bird wing
cut 2 pieces

USING PATTERNS

> Patterns help you cut out exact shapes when making crafts.

> Use tape or pins to attach the pattern to the cloth before you start cutting.

> When cutting out a shape, cut around the shape first, then make smaller cuts.

> When cutting with scissors, move the piece of cloth instead of the scissors.

> Make sure you keep your fingers out of the way while cutting. Ask an adult for help if needed.

Trace the pattern.

Cut the pattern out.

Attach the pattern to the cloth.

Cut the cloth along the pattern lines.

30

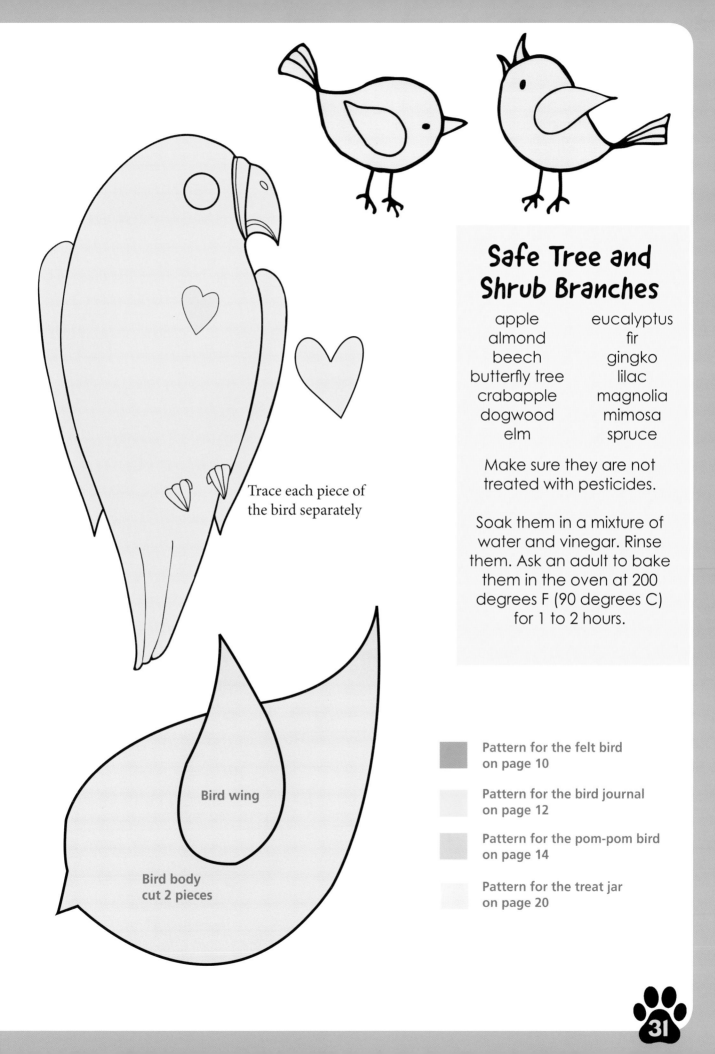

Trace each piece of the bird separately

Safe Tree and Shrub Branches

apple	eucalyptus
almond	fir
beech	gingko
butterfly tree	lilac
crabapple	magnolia
dogwood	mimosa
elm	spruce

Make sure they are not treated with pesticides.

Soak them in a mixture of water and vinegar. Rinse them. Ask an adult to bake them in the oven at 200 degrees F (90 degrees C) for 1 to 2 hours.

Bird wing

Bird body
cut 2 pieces

Pattern for the felt bird
on page 10

Pattern for the bird journal
on page 12

Pattern for the pom-pom bird
on page 14

Pattern for the treat jar
on page 20

Glossary

carabiner A metal loop with an opening that can be closed securely

hope chest A space for storing items you hope to use someday.

permanent marker A waterproof marker

pony beads A plastic barrel-shaped bead

working end The part of the rope being used to tie a knot

For More Information

Further Reading

Kuskowski, Alex. *Super Simple Pet Critter Crafts*. Minneapolis, MN: Super Sandcastle, 2017.

Mead, Wendy. *Kids Top 10 Pet Birds*. Berkeley Heights, NJ: Enslow Elementary, 2015.

Websites

Pet Birds
www.dkfindout.com/us/animals-and-nature/pet-care/pet-birds
Find out more about pet birds here.

Tropical and Exotic Birds
easyscienceforkids.com/all-about-tropical-and-exotic-birds/
This site has lots of facts about some of the kinds of birds people keep as pets, as well as other exotic birds.

Index